Last Call

Also by David Elsasser

Taking Flight: A Word Path to the Clouds
New York City: Parkside Poets Press, 2020

Delicious
New York City: NoNet Press, 2014

Last Call

Poems by
David M. Elsasser

POETS WEAR PRADA • Hoboken, New Jersey

Last Call

Poets Wear Prada
533 Bloomfield Street
Second Floor
Hoboken, New Jersey 07030.
http://pwpbooks.blogspot.com/

David Elsasser can be reached by email addressed to elsasserdavid@gmail.com.

Grateful acknowledgment is made to the following publications where some of these poems have previously appeared:

Times Square Shout Out, Soul Fountain, and *Dinner With The Muse, the Anthology of the Green Pavilion Poetry Event.*

First North American Publication 2009
First Mass Market Paperback Edition 2020

ISBN-13: 978-0-981767-88-8

Printed in the U.S.A.

Front Cover Photo: "Khami" by David M. Elsasser
Author's Photo: Su Polo

For Karyn,
who is my constant muse & inspiration
& for my daughters,
Jennifer and Emily,
who never stop making me proud

Contents

Last Call

Semicentennial

A new outlook arrives, surprise
for your fiftieth birthday.
Maybe you let it lie awhile
but you have to open it —
you can't delay long.

It's like the old days —
promptly at eighteen they found me.
"Greetings," Uncle Sam said
familiar as pain
and serious as breath itself.

Fifty. It's that half-a-century thing —
the long look back —
eternity in shrink-wrap
but maybe thirty, forty more
still smiling up unseen
past where rails meet.

All those tracks switched —
decisions and neglects —
your rickety Pullman car of cronies
rumbles up the main line toward tomorrow,
big board lit up with connections,

back to wheel's first rounding.
It's all right there —
cobblers, midwives, vagabonds —
those wayfarers of the ages
untying your bow, your gift wrap
singing your name.

Cornucopia

What you get is seldom what you planned.
The high road loops around and spills you low
before you have the ripened fruit in hand.

I could count on the fingers of one hand
the times I wound up where I meant to go —
what you get is seldom what you planned.

Cherries Jubilee would have been so grand
but I couldn't get my fruit carts in a row
before sweet juice cascaded through my hands.

So hard-earned wage or tempting contraband
read the small print by that victorious glow —
be ready with plan B if what you planned

turns from Eden into desert sand.
And when you land in that mud-filled furrow —
golden apple inches from your right hand —

realize it's what you get for your demand
that satisfaction comes in one smooth flow.
What you get is seldom what you planned —
try to break your fall with fruitful hands.

Marooned

Cubicle-free, horizon
lapsing in and out of fog —
all my life I've wanted to be here,
slipped through the hourglass chute,
time's grit a stardust field
spread before my pen, and
nature flexing every fine line.
Sun making molasses-brown beans of me —
no way back to dollars and sense.
Mine — the ceaseless ripples,
the gulls' squawk, the hooked barb
waiting to be picked clean.
Ah, the good life. So what
if sun gives me headaches,
sun and gulls' heedless clam smashing.
Even being marooned isn't perfect.
I slip another poem into
my sand chair's secret drawer,
my glass beckoning —
cool enough but not frosty.
Speech-combing gleans
all shores clean —
so where better to wash up?

she half shouts, half purrs. Purring, it seems, directly into each of our ears. Maybe that's the sign of a really good bartender. Or maybe it's magic. Maybe we hear important messages through one great generational ear somewhere. Personally I suspect it's the one hanging on a neon sign on Varick Street. An oracle hidden in plain sight. But I get funny ideas.

The barkeep needs us to know she's on our side. She'd give us the universe. Only time is growing short. Oh, it's not up yet. There's still time for one more good go-round. One great draft of life. But we have nowhere near as much future as we once did. You know, back in those bygone days when we believed in forever. Our forever. No one could tell us differently. Though of course they tried.

Now there's only a finger-thickness of tape left on the feeder spool. We hear Kate starting to warm up in the back room. The bartender senses us growing sullen. She pulls off her beer-soaked sweatshirt and liberates her pony-tail from her trucker-cap strap. She wriggles out of her jeans and jumps up on the bar, shaking her long hair free.

She is wearing only the G-string she stores in a shot glass behind the bar for emergencies. She smiles eternal bliss at us, holding the large print version of the bar menu chest high. Music blares. Her gyrations follow the beat. We all get the message.

All possibility gapes before us, on the menu. So what to go for? Her dance goes on. And on. She is Artemis, Isis, Mary, promising our resurgence. One and then another, and then another of us starts singing with the music. Only everyone is singing a different song. We sing the song we hear. Our song.

What a decision we face. For starters, there's the Pleasure Punch Cocktail, there's the Major Life-Swing Margarita, the Inner-Seeking Micro Brew, and the Wistful Manhattan.

I should stop, right here and now. There are so many more choices. You go over it for yourself. I know what I want. Oh, and by the way, I had a conversation with the bartender earlier. She says that forever isn't all that wonderful; you get so tired of yourself. Not to mention human bile and destruction.

So savor your sunset libations. This is the part she likes, she says — mixing, making eye contact, watching our breath come and go. She takes our orders. We all move along.

What Crows Tell Me

The crows come swooping
into my apartment-complex canyon
squawking their contempt for us.
"See our inky wings flexed
joyfully against the sky," they say,
"We are beauty.
You mock us with your foul asphalt
smothering the living soil so far
the rain finds nowhere to run off
and floods your streets until
your sewers back up into them.
Heed us, for your time grows short.
Today your boundless waste
swells our numbers, blackening the sky.
Tomorrow we may build our nests inside
the remnants of your rotted skyscrapers.
And even if you get lucky and survive
a while, don't be too proud. The world
was much better before you came
and all the fuss and flap you raise
won't grow you feathers
or make your plucked skins fly.
True, we are loud and brash, like you
but you are the spoilers —
we, just the reckoning."

The Game

My shoulders slumped more
with each passing,
family and friends,
I easily imagine them
shoulder perched,
spirit legs carelessly dangling,
since they whisper incessantly in my ear.
Oh, I don't mind. It's the natural order,
and they have nowhere to go.
I take them in, find them seats
these retired players,
new fans in the grandstand.
They hoot, root their teams
in turn or in chorus.
Sometimes they're a nuisance
insisting on a play I oppose
or arguing among themselves
till I step in, blow the whistle
and remind them I'm in charge now.
They usually smirk, whisper: *Just wait.*
I know what they mean. The raw deal.
The bum contract Adam and Eve bargained —
in the end you come down to a blurb:
you live, you die, your stuff goes to the curb,
you fill the ears of everyone who loved you
until, inevitably, they're called out too.

Ghosts

It is truth spared from youth, like mortality,
in fact a corollary: there are no ghosts
we tell them, only palette shifts
from red and blue to white. Only
empty wind-rocked chairs, squeaking.
Only clear windows quickly clouded over.
But time teaches us better; of course
there are ghosts. No, not clanking chains,
not hand-held heads, not squishy ectoplasm
sliming disbelievers, but plain if
less dramatic signs, everywhere: There —
daughter arranges flowers
with grandpa's hands.
There — nephew displays
great-uncle's forgotten mannerisms.
What? These aren't ghosts,
aren't even frightening, you say?
Wait till you've seen Dad stare
from morning mirror, heard
Mom's admonishments leave your lips.
Give it time. They'll fill all your haunts.
Family will spot you
in the now unborn, someday,
winding your way down
to deliver a new day.

Deer Crossing

Whimsically the world spins,
mortality making doe-eyes from curbside.
All the while your camera's running.
If you're lucky you make peace,
learn some ancestors' names and ways,
before both parents are no more
than cloud-shifts across your mind's sky,
and you plop in the driver's seat
of a rental car commercial.

Out into the traffic circle of middle age
your wheels squeal,
next generation squabbling in the back seat
screaming every time you miss a turn.

Afternoon's long green straightaway
is small challenge, but just every so often
life leaps headlong from the shoulder —
a sudden arc
across your hurtle toward tomorrow,
as foot to brake
you ride the rapids in your blood
smelling fear and asbestos.

Fate's taut haunches fly before your windshield
while you do the math of life and death,
and all your detours rapid replay
in one great leap of wonder.

Closing the Circle

"Who must die, must die in the dark, even
though she sells candles."
— Traditional Colombian proverb

Your long day closing,
I watched you dip lower
less and less mother
of lifelong memory
but refusing disappearance.
Eyes gone dark, legs still
you elbowed the horizon down
with each drop, your twilight
arresting night so long you seemed
far more flickering streetlight
than plummeting star.
Life stretched next-breath thin,
your endurance breathed faith in me
leaving me blank when you vanished.
It made sense eventually —
no image
where nothing remained
that long black month
until I dreamed you young,
childhood-morning mother
walking through night's vestibule.
You weren't just falling
all that time you said,
you were closing the circle —
bringing memory 'round.

Deep Water

We were the ark's rejects, looking
for high ground during the flood.

We hung together like lamppost drunks
trying to cast light on failed marriages.

Paths led everywhere when water receded —
tendrils found light along endless streams.

You'd be tied up when I called,
when you called back I'd be away.

Seventeen years flickered
in a handful of failed reunions;

we were always going to get together —
I only caught up when your steps ended.

Today someone solemnly tries to pin you down:
you were magpie, seeker, oddball, and helper.

Not a bad start. But artificial light
casts your reflection out ahead of me

dancing toward deep water
rippling away.

Flea Market Razor

Not some curvy plastic cutting edge
but a thing gone missing —
true-mettle longevity
still adjustable to every outgrowth.
Sure, some dead man's castoff probably
collecting dust in secondhand's back row —
like all possessions, slowly migrating
to other hands. And here now,
in stubble-rubbing contemplation,
I recall relatives obstinately saying
record player for turntable,
unable to reject any thingamajig
that still went round for them.
I hope age hasn't yet spun me
from innovation's orbit but
my disposability too plain
I seek some act, some place
with no new thing
to make me more or better.
I find this bygone handle
sure and natural, a hope
that there is finally
something to hold onto.

Voyage

For Dan Cheifetz, whose favorite song was the
Bahamian folk song "The John B. Sails"

Our workshop is labor
plied in open water
a longboat rocked by swells.
We tug oars thoughtfully
giving words time, crest
and sink on every metaphor.
And then we dock. Always
there's next week, we think.

But sometimes sails are rigged.
Wind's change whistles
someone's departure song
for us to sing right then
but we don't understand.
Or maybe we just won't believe
they're leaving for good.

So hoist up the John B. sails.
See how the mainsail sets.
Sometimes you wind up
in the drink, floundering for yourself
or you're a small boat, violently tossed
by another's surrender to the waves.
Call for the captain ashore.

We always want more time.
The captain comes aboard,
his cap pushed back,
the ship sails off.
Every sailor, knight, and
orphan finds his berth.
A journey done.
A chorus beached
to chant the verses later.

Keeping Score

Childhood counted happily
each year a gold star,
a higher score
totaled on the abacus
of hands and feet.
But having twice tallied
my sum of fingers and toes,
age became abstraction as
chronology's merriment ceased.

If yet some core of simple joy
survived, central in my fiber
the third score was no charm —
all the little piggies dread
being ham sandwiches
and shrink from touch.
They won't uncurl their tales
stubbornly remaining mum.

Where to seek one's self
when time isn't telling?
Maybe turn tree doctor,
study my limb's slant
on the family arbor,
prod every annual ring
circled around birth's
dank, vital center, peering
with hindsight.

So here I am
guilty of youth-green envy —
wanting to roll in wildflowers,
dig fingers and toes into dirt,
measure my acorn's travel
from tradition's
trunk.
I'm adding and reaching,
stubbornly resisting repetition's gravity.

Forget It

Never one to easily retrieve
facts plunked casually
into memory's reservoir,
I've always circled blocks
seeking my parked car,
circled arguments
seeking my lost point,
while circumstance
digests intention's detour.

Memory leaks sprung
way back when, well
who can remember —
don't send me hobbling off
wooden shoed
to plug recollection's dikes
with each new rivulet.
I tie no memory strings,
needing fingers free
when fate burps
and surroundings fall.
I flee chaos on bare feet.

Better to be a back-flipping flake
with instinct to shelter in
doorways of collapsing situations
than six feet under rubble,
perfectly recalling
what once stood where.
So let cognitive incontinence
dribble away. I stand
ready to surf the spill.

A Bouquet for Age

So many springs ago when I was young
and saw the fresh blooms playful in the breeze
I surged with want to pick them there among
robins hunting earthworms. On bended knees
I'd grip as many as my greedy hands
could snip or lop or manage to uproot.
I thought it wasn't time for moral plans.
I thought that blossoms were just pretty loot.
But now in later years my eye can fill
desire's vase without the need to pluck
and merely seeing beauty is a thrill —
let's say I'm spirit focused, and in luck.
I smile and walk and let the new buds be
and they smile back and flower, just for me.

Here's to There

Friends from Long-Haired Long Ago
land of fabled luster
we keep our used-to-bees together
buzzing through collective memory
from a hive beneath the bar —
that song that told it all
we sang about the journey
and the night, the company of lovers,
the laughs we laughed
together young. The heads of youth
worn nubby with the telling.

Time's a funny place, really
the distant-ever-near we travel
sending lonesome postcards home
sometimes staying long enough
to file for residency, but always
moving on before we know.
Usually soon as saying *here*
we're somewhere else
chasing recollections' swarm
or running from its sting.

Indian Summer

My eye grows subtle
perceiving reds and golds
more resonant than
eager greens that
sparked me early on.

These late warm days
more scintillating than
the long season
of sweat-soaked nights
my hand steadies
and moves slow.
Taking in the tumbling dance
of fine-veined leaves
my heart beats glad.

Acknowledgments

The author gratefully acknowledges the publications in which the following poems first appeared:

"*Last Call,*" *Times Square Shout Out*, Saturday, March 3, 2007.

"Forget It," *Soul Fountain*, Spring 2007.

"What Crows Tell Me," *Dinner With The Muse, the Anthology of the Green Pavilion Poetry Event*, Ra Rays Press, 2009.

Thanks to Khami Pellegrino, singer-songwriter, and longtime bartender at Nightingale Lounge, for posing for the cover photo.

ABOUT THE TYPE

Text for this book is set in Bookman Old Style, designed by Ong Chong Wah (b. 1955) for Monotype and released in 1990. The Malaysian-born graphic and font designer studied and worked in England, mostly in advertising prior to Monotype. His credits also include the ever-popular Footlight (Monotype) and Ocean Sans (Adobe) among a total of nine type families.

Ong's Bookman Old Style is characterized by the near-vertical stress of its face, heavy type color, wide letters, and the somewhat taller lowercase characteristic of hymn and classic children's books. Ong based his digitized design on various 1960s and 1970s phototypesetting revivals of Alexander Phemister's classic Old Style Antique (circa 1858) cut for the Miller and Richard foundry in Edinburgh, Scotland, as a "modern" recasting of the Caslon typeface cut by William Caslon in the 1720s.

Despite the "Old Style" tag and look — or perhaps because of it — Ong's design continues to prevail. Title designer Victoria Vaus selected Bookman Old Style for the main title of the 1999 film *Election*, a high school comedy starring Matthew Broderick and Reese Witherspoon, directed by Alexander Payne. Later the typeface was adopted for the original Tumblr logo (2007–2013) by designer Peter Vidani — prior to Yahoo! acquisition mid-2013. Bookman Old Style was chosen here for its legibility, classic storybook styling, and general good humor.